Mexican Rice Cookbook 101

Classic and Creative Recipes for Authentic Mexican Rice Dishes

While every precaution has been taken in the preparation of this book, the publisher assumes no responsibility for errors or omissions, or for damages resulting from the use of the information contained herein.

MEXICAN RICE COOKBOOK 101

First edition. November 11, 2023.

Copyright © 2023 john ahmad.

ISBN: 979-8223628279

Written by john ahmad.

John Ahmad

Chapter Outline:

1. **Introduction to Mexican Rice**

- Brief history and cultural significance
- Essential ingredients and equipment for cooking Mexican rice

1. **Traditional Mexican Rice Recipes**

- Arroz Rojo (Red Rice)
- Arroz Verde (Green Rice)
- Arroz a la Mexicana (Mexican-style Rice)
- Arroz Amarillo (Yellow Rice)

1. **Flavored and Infused Rice Variations**

- Cilantro Lime Rice
- Chipotle Rice
- Garlic Butter Rice
- Tomato and Chilies Rice

1. **One-Pot Rice Meals**

- Arroz con Pollo (Chicken and Rice)
- Arroz con Camarones (Shrimp and Rice)
- Vegetarian Rice Skillet
- Chorizo and Rice Skillet

1. **Rice Side Dishes and Salads**

- Mexican Rice Pudding
- Fiesta Rice Salad
- Avocado Lime Rice

- Roasted Corn and Black Bean Rice

1. **Street Food Inspired Rice Recipes**

- Mexican Rice Burritos
- Rice-stuffed Empanadas
- Rice Tamales
- Rice-stuffed Bell Peppers

1. **Rice Soups and Stews**

- Sopa de Arroz (Mexican Rice Soup)
- Caldo de Res (Beef and Rice Soup)
- Pozole Rojo with Rice
- Chicken and Rice Pozole

1. **Rice-based Casseroles and Bakes**

- Chiles Rellenos Casserole
- Enchilada Rice Casserole
- Chicken and Rice Enmoladas
- Rice and Bean Bake

1. **Festive and Holiday Rice Dishes**

- Arroz Navideño (Christmas Rice)
- Day of the Dead Rice
- Rice-stuffed Poblanos (Chiles en Nogada)
- Traditional Rice Tamales

1. **Rice Desserts and Sweet Treats**

- Horchata Rice Pudding
- Arroz con Leche Ice Cream

- Caramelized Rice Flan
- Rice Krispies Mexican Treats

1. **Modern and Fusion Rice Creations**

- Mexican Rice Sushi Rolls
- Rice-stuffed Peppers with Quinoa
- Tex-Mex Rice and Beans Bowl
- Mexican Rice Pizza

1. **Tips and Techniques for Perfect Mexican Rice**

- Preparing and toasting rice for maximum flavor
- Achieving the right texture and consistency
- Seasoning and spice combinations
- Storage and reheating recommendations

1. **Beyond the Rice: Complementary Mexican Dishes**

- Guacamole and Salsa Variations
- Traditional Mexican Sides and Appetizers
- Refreshing Agua Fresca Recipes
- Mexican-inspired Cocktails and Mocktails

Chapter 1: Introduction to Mexican Rice

Mexican rice, also known as "arroz Mexicano" or "arroz rojo," is a staple dish in Mexican cuisine. It is a flavorful and versatile rice preparation that has gained popularity around the world. In this chapter, we will delve into the rich history and cultural significance of Mexican rice, as well as explore the essential ingredients and equipment needed to create delicious and authentic Mexican rice dishes.

1.1 The Rich History of Mexican Rice

Mexican rice has a fascinating history that dates back centuries. The origins of Mexican rice can be traced to the Spanish colonization of Mexico in the 16th century. The Spaniards introduced rice to the region, which quickly assimilated into the local cuisine. Over time, Mexican cooks infused their own unique flavors and techniques into the rice, resulting in the creation of distinct Mexican rice recipes.

Mexican rice became deeply embedded in Mexican culture, and it is now considered a beloved dish in traditional celebrations, family gatherings, and everyday meals. Its vibrant colors, aromatic spices, and satisfying flavors make it a standout component of Mexican gastronomy.

1.2 Cultural Significance of Mexican Rice

Mexican rice holds a special place in Mexican culture, often symbolizing unity, hospitality, and celebration. It is a common sight on festive occasions, such as weddings, birthdays, and religious festivals. The vibrant red, green, and yellow hues of the rice evoke a sense of joy and excitement, adding visual appeal to the dining experience.

Sharing a meal that includes Mexican rice is a way of bringing people together, fostering a sense of community and connection. It is often served alongside other traditional Mexican dishes, such as tacos, enchiladas, and tamales, creating a harmonious culinary experience that reflects the diversity and richness of Mexican cuisine.

1.3 Essential Ingredients for Cooking Mexican Rice

To prepare authentic Mexican rice, it is important to have the right ingredients that capture the essence of the dish. Here are some key ingredients commonly used in Mexican rice recipes:

1.3.1 Rice Varieties:

Long-grain white rice: This is the most commonly used rice variety for Mexican rice. Its firm texture and ability to absorb flavors make it ideal for creating fluffy and flavorful rice dishes.

1.3.2 Aromatics and Vegetables:

Onion: A staple ingredient that adds depth and flavor to the rice.

Garlic: Provides a savory note and enhances the overall taste.

Tomatoes: Fresh or canned tomatoes are often used to give the rice its vibrant red color and tangy taste.

Bell peppers: green or red bell peppers add a hint of sweetness and a pleasant crunch.

1.3.3 Spices and Seasonings:

Cumin: A warm and earthy spice that imparts a distinct Mexican flavor.

Paprika or chili powder: Adds a touch of smokiness and mild heat to the rice.

Mexican oregano: Known for its unique flavor profile, Mexican oregano adds a hint of citrus and complexity to the dish.

Bay leaves: Fragrant leaves that infuse the rice with a subtle aromatic essence.

1.3.4 Broth or Stock:

Chicken or vegetable broth: Used as the cooking liquid for the rice, providing a savory base and enhancing the overall flavor.

1.4 Equipment for Cooking Mexican Rice

Having the right equipment can greatly assist in achieving the perfect texture and flavor for your Mexican rice. Here are some essential kitchen tools you will need:

1.4.1 Medium-Sized Pot:

A medium-sized, heavy-bottomed pot with a tight-fitting lid is essential for cooking Mexican rice. It ensures even heat distribution and prevents the rice from sticking or burning.

1.4.2 Wooden Spoon or Spatula:

A wooden spoon or spatula is ideal for stirring and fluffing the rice without damaging the grains.

1.4.3 Knife and Cutting Board:

These tools are necessary for chopping onions, garlic, tomatoes, and other vegetables.

1.4.4 Measuring Cups and Spoons:

Accurate measuring of ingredients is crucial for consistent and balanced flavors in your Mexican rice.

By understanding the history, cultural significance, essential ingredients, and equipment, you are now equipped with the foundational knowledge to embark on a flavorful journey through the world of Mexican rice. In the following chapters, we will explore a variety of traditional recipes, innovative variations, and useful techniques to help you create delicious Mexican rice dishes that will impress your family and friends.

Chapter 2: Traditional Mexican Rice Recipes

Mexican cuisine is renowned for its vibrant and flavorful rice dishes. In this chapter, we will explore four classic traditional Mexican rice recipes that have stood the test of time. These recipes will take you on a culinary journey through the colors, aromas, and tastes that define Mexican rice. From the rich and savory Arroz Rojo to the fresh and herbaceous Arroz Verde, get ready to tantalize your taste buds with these beloved Mexican rice variations.

2.1 Arroz Rojo (Red Rice)

Arroz Rojo, or red rice, is a staple in Mexican households. This vibrant and aromatic dish gets its characteristic red color from the combination of tomatoes, onions, and spices. The flavors are rich, with a slight tanginess that pairs perfectly with a variety of main dishes.

Ingredients:

- 1 cup long-grain white rice
- 2 tablespoons vegetable oil
- 1/2 onion, finely chopped
- 2 cloves garlic, minced
- 2 ripe tomatoes, diced
- 1 teaspoon ground cumin
- 1 teaspoon paprika
- 2 cups chicken or vegetable broth
- Salt, to taste
- Fresh cilantro, chopped (for garnish)

Instructions:

1. Rinse the rice under cold water until the water runs clear. Drain and set aside.

2. Heat the vegetable oil in a medium-sized pot over medium heat. Add the chopped onion and minced garlic. Sauté until the onion becomes translucent.
3. Add the diced tomatoes, cumin, and paprika to the pot. Cook for 5 minutes, allowing the tomatoes to soften and release their juices.
4. Add the rice to the pot and stir well, ensuring that the grains are coated with the tomato mixture.
5. Pour in the chicken or vegetable broth and season with salt to taste. Stir gently to combine.
6. Bring the mixture to a boil, then reduce the heat to low. Cover the pot with a tight-fitting lid and simmer for about 20-25 minutes, or until the rice is tender and the liquid is absorbed.
7. Once cooked, fluff the rice with a fork and let it sit, covered, for a few minutes.
8. Serve the Arroz Rojo garnished with freshly chopped cilantro. It pairs well with a variety of Mexican main dishes such as enchiladas, carne asada, or grilled chicken.

2.2 Arroz Verde (Green Rice)

Arroz Verde, or green rice, is a delightful variation that showcases the vibrant flavors of fresh herbs like cilantro and parsley. This aromatic and verdant rice is a perfect complement to grilled meats, seafood, or vegetarian dishes.

Ingredients:

- 1 cup long-grain white rice
- 1 ½ cups chicken or vegetable broth
- 1 cup packed fresh cilantro leaves
- 1/2 cup packed fresh parsley leaves
- 1 jalapeño or serrano pepper, seeds removed
- 1/2 onion, roughly chopped
- 2 cloves garlic
- 1 tablespoon lime juice
- Salt, to taste
- 2 tablespoons vegetable oil

Instructions:

1. In a blender or food processor, combine the cilantro, parsley, jalapeño or serrano pepper, onion, garlic, lime juice, and a pinch of salt. Blend until you have a smooth, vibrant green mixture. Set aside.
2. Rinse the rice under cold water until the water runs clear. Drain and set aside.
3. Heat the vegetable oil in a medium-sized pot over medium heat. Add the rice and sauté for a few minutes until it becomes translucent.
4. Pour the green herb mixture into the pot and stir well to coat the rice evenly.
5. Add the chicken or vegetable broth and season with salt to taste. Stir gently to combine.

6. Bring the mixture to a boil, then reduce the heat to low. Cover the pot with a tight-fitting lid and simmer for about 20-25 minutes, or until the rice is tender and the liquid is absorbed.

7. Once cooked, fluff the rice with a fork and let it sit, covered, for a few minutes.

8. Serve the Arroz Verde as a vibrant and flavorful side dish alongside grilled meats, fish, or your favorite Mexican-inspired entrées.

2.3 Arroz a la Mexicana (Mexican-style Rice)

Arroz a la Mexicana, or Mexican-style rice, is a beloved classic that combines the flavors of tomatoes, onions, and garlic. This versatile dish is a staple in Mexican households and can be enjoyed as a side dish or as a base for heartier rice-based meals.

Ingredients:

- 1 cup long-grain white rice
- 2 tablespoons vegetable oil
- 1/2 onion, finely chopped
- 2 cloves garlic, minced
- 2 ripe tomatoes, diced
- 1 ¾ cups chicken or vegetable broth
- Salt, to taste

Instructions:

1. Rinse the rice under cold water until the water runs clear. Drain and set aside.
2. Heat the vegetable oil in a medium-sized pot over medium heat. Add the chopped onion and minced garlic. Sauté until the onion becomes translucent.
3. Add the diced tomatoes to the pot and cook for a few minutes until they start to soften.
4. Add the rice to the pot and stir well, ensuring that the grains are coated with the tomato mixture.
5. Pour in the chicken or vegetable broth and season with salt to taste. Stir gently to combine.
6. Bring the mixture to a boil, then reduce the heat to low. Cover the pot with a tight-fitting lid and simmer for about 20-25 minutes, or until the rice is tender and the liquid is absorbed.
7. Once cooked, fluff the rice with a fork and let it sit, covered, for a few minutes.

8. Serve the Arroz a la Mexicana alongside your favorite Mexican dishes, such as tacos, fajitas, or grilled vegetables.

2.4 Arroz Amarillo (Yellow Rice)

Arroz Amarillo, or yellow rice, is a vibrant and fragrant dish that gets its beautiful golden color from the use of saffron or turmeric. This flavorful rice is commonly served alongside a variety of Mexican and Latin American dishes.

Ingredients:

- 1 cup long-grain white rice
- 2 tablespoons vegetable oil
- 1/2 onion, finely chopped
- 2 cloves garlic, minced
- 1 teaspoon ground turmeric or a pinch of saffron threads
- 1 ¾ cups chicken or vegetable broth
- Salt, to taste

Instructions:

1. Rinse the rice under cold water until the water runs clear. Drain and set aside.
2. Heat the vegetable oil in a medium-sized pot over medium heat. Add the chopped onion and minced garlic. Sauté until the onion becomes translucent.
3. Add the ground turmeric or saffron threads to the pot and stir well to release their color and aroma.
4. Add the rice to the pot and stir well, ensuring that the grains are coated with the turmeric or saffron mixture.
5. Pour in the chicken or vegetable broth and season with salt to taste. Stir gently to combine.
6. Bring the mixture to a boil, then reduce the heat to low. Cover the pot with a tight-fitting lid and simmer for about 20-25 minutes, or until the rice is tender and the liquid is absorbed.
7. Once cooked, fluff the rice with a fork and let it sit, covered, for a few minutes.

8. Serve the Arroz Amarillo as a vibrant and aromatic side dish alongside your favorite Mexican or Latin American meals.

In the next chapters, we will explore exciting variations of Mexican rice recipes, including vegetarian, seafood, and meat-based options, allowing you to expand your culinary repertoire and continue your flavorful journey through the world of Mexican rice.

Chapter 3: Flavored and Infused Rice Variations

In addition to the traditional Mexican rice recipes, there are numerous delicious variations that add unique flavors and twists to this beloved dish. In this chapter, we will explore four flavorful and aromatic rice variations: Cilantro Lime Rice, Chipotle Rice, Garlic Butter Rice, and Tomato and Chilies Rice. These recipes will elevate your Mexican rice experience and provide an exciting range of flavors to suit your preferences.

3.1 Cilantro Lime Rice

Cilantro Lime Rice is a zesty and refreshing variation that combines the bright flavors of cilantro and lime. It pairs perfectly with grilled meats, seafood, or as a filling for burritos and tacos.

Ingredients:

- 1 cup long-grain white rice
- 1 ¾ cups chicken or vegetable broth
- 2 tablespoons fresh lime juice
- ¼ cup fresh cilantro, finely chopped
- Salt, to taste

Instructions:

1. Rinse the rice under cold water until the water runs clear. Drain and set aside.
2. In a medium-sized pot, combine the rice and broth. Bring to a boil over high heat.
3. Once boiling, reduce the heat to low, cover the pot with a tight-fitting lid, and simmer for about 20-25 minutes, or until the rice is tender and the liquid is absorbed.
4. Remove the pot from heat and let it sit, covered, for a few minutes.
5. Fluff the rice with a fork, then add the fresh lime juice and chopped cilantro. Stir gently to combine.
6. Season with salt to taste.
7. Serve the Cilantro Lime Rice as a vibrant and tangy side dish or as a base for your favorite Mexican-inspired meals.

3.2 Chipotle Rice

Chipotle Rice is a smoky and slightly spicy variation that adds a depth of flavor to your Mexican rice. The smokiness of chipotle peppers combined with the richness of spices creates a delicious and satisfying dish.

Ingredients:

- 1 cup long-grain white rice
- 1 ¾ cups chicken or vegetable broth
- 1 chipotle pepper in adobo sauce, finely chopped
- 1 teaspoon adobo sauce (from the chipotle pepper can)
- ½ teaspoon ground cumin
- ½ teaspoon paprika
- Salt, to taste

Instructions:

1. Rinse the rice under cold water until the water runs clear. Drain and set aside.
2. In a medium-sized pot, combine the rice, broth, chipotle pepper, adobo sauce, cumin, paprika, and a pinch of salt.
3. Bring the mixture to a boil over high heat.
4. Once boiling, reduce the heat to low, cover the pot with a tight-fitting lid, and simmer for about 20-25 minutes, or until the rice is tender and the liquid is absorbed.
5. Remove the pot from heat and let it sit, covered, for a few minutes.
6. Fluff the rice with a fork.
7. Serve the Chipotle Rice as a bold and flavorful side dish alongside grilled meats, roasted vegetables, or as a filling for burritos and bowls.

3.3 Garlic Butter Rice

Garlic Butter Rice is a simple yet irresistible variation that adds richness and depth to your Mexican rice. The combination of garlic and butter creates a luxurious and comforting dish that is sure to please.

Ingredients:

- 1 cup long-grain white rice
- 1 ¾ cups chicken or vegetable broth
- 2 tablespoons unsalted butter
- 3 cloves garlic, minced
- Salt, to taste

Instructions:

1. Rinse the rice under cold water until the water runs clear. Drain and set aside.
2. In a medium-sized pot, melt the butter over medium heat.
3. Add the minced garlic to the pot and sauté for a minute until fragrant.
4. Add the rice to the pot and stir well, ensuring that the grains are coated with the garlic-infused butter.
5. Pour in the chicken or vegetable broth and season with salt to taste. Stir gently to combine.
6. Bring the mixture to a boil over high heat.
7. Once boiling, reduce the heat to low, cover the pot with a tight-fitting lid, and simmer for about 20-25 minutes, or until the rice is tender and the liquid is absorbed.
8. Remove the pot from heat and let it sit, covered, for a few minutes.
9. Fluff the rice with a fork.
10. Serve the Garlic Butter Rice as a comforting and flavorful side dish alongside a variety of Mexican-inspired meals.

3.4 Tomato and Chilies Rice

Tomato and Chilies Rice is a vibrant and flavorful variation that combines the tanginess of tomatoes with the mild heat of chilies. This rice pairs well with grilled meats, enchiladas, or as a filling for stuffed peppers.

Ingredients:

- 1 cup long-grain white rice
- 1 ¾ cups chicken or vegetable broth
- 2 tablespoons vegetable oil
- ½ onion, finely chopped
- 2 cloves garlic, minced
- 1 jalapeño or serrano pepper, seeds removed and finely chopped
- 2 ripe tomatoes, diced
- 1 teaspoon ground cumin
- Salt, to taste

Instructions:

1. Rinse the rice under cold water until the water runs clear. Drain and set aside.
2. In a medium-sized pot, heat the vegetable oil over medium heat.
3. Add the chopped onion, minced garlic, and chopped jalapeño or serrano pepper to the pot. Sauté until the onion becomes translucent and the peppers soften.
4. Add the diced tomatoes and ground cumin to the pot. Cook for a few minutes until the tomatoes release their juices and soften.
5. Add the rice to the pot and stir well, ensuring that the grains are coated with the tomato and chili mixture.
6. Pour in the chicken or vegetable broth and season with salt to

taste. Stir gently to combine.

7. Bring the mixture to a boil over high heat.

8. Once boiling, reduce the heat to low, cover the pot with a tight-fitting lid, and simmer for about 20-25 minutes, or until the rice is tender and the liquid is absorbed.

9. Remove the pot from heat and let it sit, covered, for a few minutes.

10. Fluff the rice with a fork.

11. Serve the Tomato and Chilies Rice as a vibrant and flavorful side dish or as a base for your favorite Mexican-inspired meals.

These flavored and infused rice variations will add a new dimension of taste and excitement to your Mexican rice repertoire. In the upcoming chapters, we will explore additional creative and delectable recipes that showcase the versatility of Mexican rice in both vegetarian and meat-based dishes.

Chapter 4: One-Pot Rice Meals

One-pot rice meals are not only convenient but also incredibly flavorful. In this chapter, we will delve into the world of delicious and satisfying one-pot rice meals. Whether you prefer chicken, shrimp, or vegetarian options, these recipes will provide you with hearty and complete meals that are easy to prepare and packed with Mexican-inspired flavors.

4.1 Arroz con Pollo (Chicken and Rice)

Arroz con Pollo, or Chicken and Rice, is a classic one-pot dish that combines tender chicken pieces with flavorful rice. This comforting and well-balanced meal is a staple in Mexican cuisine.

Ingredients:

- 2 tablespoons vegetable oil
- 4 bone-in chicken thighs (or your preferred chicken parts)
- 1 onion, finely chopped
- 2 cloves garlic, minced
- 1 bell pepper, diced
- 1 cup long-grain white rice
- 1 ¾ cups chicken broth
- 1 teaspoon ground cumin
- 1 teaspoon paprika
- Salt and pepper, to taste
- Fresh cilantro, chopped (for garnish)

Instructions:

1. Heat the vegetable oil in a large skillet or Dutch oven over medium-high heat.
2. Add the chicken thighs to the skillet and cook until browned on both sides. Remove the chicken from the skillet and set aside.

3. In the same skillet, add the chopped onion, minced garlic, and diced bell pepper. Sauté until the vegetables soften and become fragrant.
4. Add the rice to the skillet and stir well to coat the grains with the vegetable mixture.
5. Pour in the chicken broth, ground cumin, paprika, salt, and pepper. Stir to combine.
6. Place the browned chicken thighs on top of the rice mixture in the skillet.
7. Bring the mixture to a boil, then reduce the heat to low. Cover the skillet with a lid and simmer for about 20-25 minutes, or until the rice is tender and the chicken is cooked through.
8. Remove the skillet from heat and let it sit, covered, for a few minutes.
9. Serve the Arroz con Pollo hot, garnished with fresh cilantro.

4.2 Arroz con Camarones (Shrimp and Rice)

Arroz con Camarones, or Shrimp and Rice, is a delightful one-pot meal that showcases the delicate flavors of shrimp combined with aromatic rice. This dish is perfect for seafood lovers and will transport you to the coastal regions of Mexico.

Ingredients:

- 2 tablespoons vegetable oil
- 1 pound shrimp, peeled and deveined
- 1 onion, finely chopped
- 2 cloves garlic, minced
- 1 bell pepper, diced
- 1 cup long-grain white rice
- 1 ¾ cups chicken or vegetable broth
- 1 teaspoon ground cumin
- 1 teaspoon paprika
- Salt and pepper, to taste
- Fresh parsley, chopped (for garnish)

Instructions:

1. Heat the vegetable oil in a large skillet or Dutch oven over medium-high heat.
2. Add the shrimp to the skillet and cook until pink and cooked through. Remove the shrimp from the skillet and set aside.
3. In the same skillet, add the chopped onion, minced garlic, and diced bell pepper. Sauté until the vegetables soften and become fragrant.
4. Add the rice to the skillet and stir well to coat the grains with the vegetable mixture.
5. Pour in the chicken or vegetable broth, ground cumin, paprika, salt, and pepper. Stir to combine.
6. Place the cooked shrimp on top of the rice mixture in the

skillet.

7. Bring the mixture to a boil, then reduce the heat to low. Cover the skillet with a lid and simmer for about 20-25 minutes, or until the rice is tender.

8. Remove the skillet from heat and let it sit, covered, for a few minutes.

9. Serve the Arroz con Camarones hot, garnished with fresh parsley.

4.3 Vegetarian Rice Skillet

For those who prefer a meatless option, the Vegetarian Rice Skillet is a delightful and nutritious one-pot meal that highlights the vibrant flavors of vegetables and spices.

Ingredients:

- 2 tablespoons vegetable oil
- 1 onion, finely chopped
- 2 cloves garlic, minced
- 1 bell pepper, diced
- 1 zucchini, diced
- 1 cup long-grain white rice
- 1 ¾ cups vegetable broth
- 1 teaspoon ground cumin
- 1 teaspoon paprika
- Salt and pepper, to taste
- Fresh cilantro, chopped (for garnish)

Instructions:

1. Heat the vegetable oil in a large skillet or Dutch oven over medium-high heat.
2. Add the chopped onion, minced garlic, diced bell pepper, and diced zucchini to the skillet. Sauté until the vegetables soften and become fragrant.
3. Add the rice to the skillet and stir well to coat the grains with the vegetable mixture.
4. Pour in the vegetable broth, ground cumin, paprika, salt, and pepper. Stir to combine.
5. Bring the mixture to a boil, then reduce the heat to low. Cover the skillet with a lid and simmer for about 20-25 minutes, or until the rice is tender.
6. Remove the skillet from heat and let it sit, covered, for a few

minutes.

7. Serve the Vegetarian Rice Skillet hot, garnished with fresh cilantro.

4.4 Chorizo and Rice Skillet

Chorizo and Rice Skillet is a flavorful and hearty one-pot meal that combines the robust flavors of chorizo sausage with aromatic rice. This dish is perfect for those who enjoy a touch of spice and a satisfying meaty component.

Ingredients:

- 2 tablespoons vegetable oil
- 8 ounces chorizo sausage, casings removed and crumbled
- 1 onion, finely chopped
- 2 cloves garlic, minced
- 1 bell pepper, diced
- 1 cup long-grain white rice
- 1 ¾ cups chicken or vegetable broth
- 1 teaspoon ground cumin
- Salt and pepper, to taste
- Fresh parsley, chopped (for garnish)

Instructions:

1. Heat the vegetable oil in a large skillet or Dutch oven over medium-high heat.
2. Add the crumbled chorizo sausage to the skillet and cook until browned and cooked through. Remove the chorizo from the skillet and set aside.
3. In the same skillet, add the chopped onion, minced garlic, and diced bell pepper. Sauté until the vegetables soften and become fragrant.
4. Add the rice to the skillet and stir well to coat the grains with the vegetable mixture.
5. Pour in the chicken or vegetable broth, ground cumin, salt, and pepper. Stir to combine.
6. Place the cooked chorizo on top of the rice mixture in the

skillet.

7. Bring the mixture to a boil, then reduce the heat to low. Cover the skillet with a lid and simmer for about 20-25 minutes, or until the rice is tender.

8. Remove the skillet from heat and let it sit, covered, for a few minutes.

9. Serve the Chorizo and Rice Skillet hot, garnished with fresh parsley.

These one-pot rice meals are perfect for busy weeknight dinners or gatherings with family and friends. They offer a complete and satisfying meal in a single dish, showcasing the versatility and deliciousness of Mexican rice.

Chapter 5: Rice Side Dishes and Salads

Rice can be transformed into delightful side dishes and refreshing salads that complement a wide range of main courses. In this chapter, we will explore a selection of flavorful rice side dishes and salads that will elevate your meals and add a touch of Mexican flair.

5.1 Mexican Rice Pudding

Mexican Rice Pudding, also known as Arroz con Leche, is a rich and comforting dessert that combines cooked rice with creamy milk, sweetened with sugar and flavored with warm spices. This traditional dessert is a favorite in Mexican cuisine.

Ingredients:

- 1 cup cooked white rice
- 2 cups whole milk
- ¼ cup granulated sugar
- 1 cinnamon stick
- 1 teaspoon vanilla extract
- Ground cinnamon, for garnish

Instructions:

1. In a saucepan, combine the cooked rice, whole milk, granulated sugar, and cinnamon stick.
2. Place the saucepan over medium heat and bring the mixture to a gentle simmer, stirring occasionally.
3. Reduce the heat to low and continue to cook, stirring frequently, for about 30-35 minutes, or until the mixture thickens and the rice is tender.
4. Remove the saucepan from heat and discard the cinnamon stick.
5. Stir in the vanilla extract.

6. Transfer the Mexican Rice Pudding to serving bowls or cups.
7. Sprinkle ground cinnamon on top for garnish.
8. Serve the Mexican Rice Pudding warm or chilled.

5.2 Fiesta Rice Salad

Fiesta Rice Salad is a vibrant and refreshing salad that combines cooked rice with an array of colorful vegetables, beans, and zesty dressing. This salad is perfect for picnics, potlucks, or as a side dish for grilled meats.

Ingredients:

- 2 cups cooked long-grain white rice
- 1 cup black beans, rinsed and drained
- 1 cup corn kernels, cooked
- 1 bell pepper, diced (any color)
- 1 small red onion, finely chopped
- 1 jalapeño pepper, seeds removed and finely chopped (optional for heat)
- ½ cup cherry tomatoes, halved
- ¼ cup fresh cilantro, chopped
- Juice of 1 lime
- 2 tablespoons olive oil
- Salt and pepper, to taste

Instructions:

1. In a large bowl, combine the cooked rice, black beans, corn kernels, diced bell pepper, chopped red onion, chopped jalapeño pepper (if using), cherry tomatoes, and chopped cilantro.
2. In a separate small bowl, whisk together the lime juice, olive oil, salt, and pepper to make the dressing.
3. Pour the dressing over the rice mixture and toss well to coat all the ingredients.
4. Adjust the seasoning if needed.
5. Cover the bowl and refrigerate for at least 30 minutes to allow the flavors to meld together.

6. Serve the Fiesta Rice Salad chilled as a refreshing and colorful
    side dish.

5.3 Avocado Lime Rice

Avocado Lime Rice is a creamy and tangy side dish that combines the smoothness of avocado with the zesty freshness of lime. This rice pairs well with grilled chicken, fish tacos, or as a filling for burritos.

Ingredients:

- 1 cup cooked long-grain white rice
- 1 ripe avocado, peeled and pitted
- Juice of 1 lime
- 2 tablespoons chopped fresh cilantro
- Salt and pepper, to taste

Instructions:

1. In a bowl, mash the ripe avocado until smooth.
2. Add the cooked rice, lime juice, chopped fresh cilantro, salt, and pepper to the bowl.
3. Stir well to combine all the ingredients and coat the rice with the avocado mixture.
4. Adjust the seasoning if needed.
5. Serve the Avocado Lime Rice at room temperature as a creamy and tangy side dish.

5.4 Roasted Corn and Black Bean Rice

Roasted Corn and Black Bean Rice is a flavorful and hearty side dish that combines the sweetness of roasted corn with the earthiness of black beans. This rice dish is a perfect accompaniment to grilled meats or as a filling for vegetarian burritos.

Ingredients:

- 1 cup cooked long-grain white rice
- 1 cup roasted corn kernels (you can use frozen roasted corn or roast fresh corn on the cob and cut off the kernels)
- 1 cup black beans, rinsed and drained
- ¼ cup diced red bell pepper
- ¼ cup diced green bell pepper
- 2 tablespoons chopped fresh cilantro
- Juice of 1 lime
- 1 tablespoon olive oil
- 1 teaspoon ground cumin
- Salt and pepper, to taste

Instructions:

1. In a large bowl, combine the cooked rice, roasted corn kernels, black beans, diced red bell pepper, diced green bell pepper, and chopped fresh cilantro.
2. In a separate small bowl, whisk together the lime juice, olive oil, ground cumin, salt, and pepper to make the dressing.
3. Pour the dressing over the rice mixture and toss well to coat all the ingredients.
4. Adjust the seasoning if needed.
5. Let the Roasted Corn and Black Bean Rice sit for about 10-15 minutes to allow the flavors to meld together.
6. Serve the rice dish at room temperature as a flavorful and satisfying side dish.

These rice side dishes and salads provide a delightful array of flavors and textures, enhancing your mealtime experience with their vibrant and refreshing qualities.

Chapter 6: Street Food Inspired Rice Recipes

Street food is a vibrant and exciting part of Mexican cuisine. In this chapter, we will explore street food-inspired rice recipes that capture the essence of Mexican flavors in portable and delicious creations. From flavorful burritos to stuffed empanadas and tamales, these recipes will transport you to the lively streets of Mexico.

6.1 Mexican Rice Burritos

Mexican Rice Burritos are hearty and satisfying street food favorites. They are filled with flavorful rice, protein of your choice, and an assortment of toppings, making them a complete meal on the go.

Ingredients:

- 1 cup cooked long-grain white rice
- 1 cup cooked protein (e.g., grilled chicken, beef, or sautéed vegetables)
- 4 large flour tortillas
- 1 cup refried beans
- ½ cup shredded cheese (e.g., cheddar or Monterey Jack)
- Toppings of your choice: salsa, guacamole, sour cream, diced tomatoes, chopped cilantro

Instructions:

1. Warm the flour tortillas in a dry skillet or microwave until they are pliable.
2. Spread a quarter of the refried beans on each tortilla.
3. Spoon a quarter of the cooked rice onto the beans.
4. Add a quarter of the cooked protein on top of the rice.
5. Sprinkle a quarter of the shredded cheese over the protein.
6. Add your desired toppings, such as salsa, guacamole, sour

cream, diced tomatoes, and chopped cilantro.

7. Roll up the tortilla tightly, tucking in the sides as you go.

8. Repeat the process with the remaining tortillas and ingredients.

9. Serve the Mexican Rice Burritos warm and enjoy the flavorful combination of rice, protein, and toppings.

6.2 Rice-stuffed Empanadas

Rice-stuffed Empanadas are delicious hand-held pastries filled with a savory mixture of rice and various ingredients. These portable treats are perfect for snacking or as a main dish in a casual gathering.

Ingredients:

- 2 cups cooked long-grain white rice
- 1 cup cooked protein or vegetables (e.g., shredded chicken, ground beef, black beans, corn)
- ½ cup diced onions
- 2 cloves garlic, minced
- 1 jalapeño pepper, seeds removed and finely chopped
- 1 teaspoon ground cumin
- Salt and pepper, to taste
- 1 package pre-made empanada dough (or homemade dough)
- Oil, for frying

Instructions:

1. In a skillet, heat some oil over medium heat. Sauté the onions, minced garlic, and jalapeño pepper until they soften and become fragrant.
2. Add the cooked protein or vegetables to the skillet and season with ground cumin, salt, and pepper. Cook for a few minutes to combine the flavors.
3. Stir in the cooked rice and continue to cook for another few minutes. Remove from heat and let the filling cool slightly.
4. Roll out the empanada dough on a floured surface to about 1/8-inch thickness.
5. Cut out circles of dough using a round cookie cutter or the rim of a glass.
6. Spoon a tablespoon of the rice filling onto one half of each dough circle.

7. Fold the other half of the dough over the filling, creating a half-moon shape.
8. Press the edges of the dough together and seal by crimping with a fork.
9. Heat oil in a deep skillet or deep fryer to about 350°F (175°C).
10. Fry the empanadas in batches until golden brown on both sides, turning them halfway through.
11. Remove the empanadas from the oil and let them drain on a paper towel-lined plate.
12. Serve the Rice-stuffed Empanadas warm and enjoy the crispy exterior and flavorful rice filling.

6.3 Rice Tamales

Rice Tamales are a unique twist on traditional tamales, featuring a filling of seasoned rice wrapped in corn husks and steamed to perfection. These handheld delights are a true representation of Mexican street food culture.

Ingredients:

- 2 cups cooked long-grain white rice
- ½ cup diced onions
- 2 cloves garlic, minced
- 1 jalapeño pepper, seeds removed and finely chopped
- 1 teaspoon ground cumin
- Salt and pepper, to taste
- Corn husks, soaked in water for at least 1 hour
- Salsa or hot sauce, for serving

Instructions:

1. In a skillet, heat some oil over medium heat. Sauté the onions, minced garlic, and jalapeño pepper until they soften and become fragrant.
2. Add the cooked rice to the skillet and season with ground cumin, salt, and pepper. Cook for a few minutes to combine the flavors. Remove from heat and let the filling cool slightly.
3. Drain the corn husks and pat them dry with a towel.
4. Take a corn husk and spread a thin layer of the rice filling on one end of the husk, leaving some space around the edges.
5. Roll the husk tightly around the filling, folding the ends inward to secure the tamale.
6. Repeat the process with the remaining husks and filling.
7. Arrange the tamales in a steamer basket, making sure they are placed upright.
8. Steam the tamales over medium-high heat for about 45

minutes to 1 hour, or until the filling is cooked through and the husks easily peel away.

9. Carefully remove the tamales from the steamer and let them cool slightly before serving.

10. Serve the Rice Tamales warm with salsa or hot sauce for added flavor.

6.4 Rice-stuffed Bell Peppers

Rice-stuffed Bell Peppers are a colorful and satisfying street food option. The bell peppers are filled with seasoned rice and baked until tender, creating a flavorful and nutritious meal.

Ingredients:

- 4 bell peppers (any color), tops removed and seeds removed
- 2 cups cooked long-grain white rice
- 1 cup cooked protein or vegetables (e.g., ground beef, shredded chicken, black beans, corn)
- ½ cup diced onions
- 2 cloves garlic, minced
- 1 jalapeño pepper, seeds removed and finely chopped
- 1 teaspoon ground cumin
- Salt and pepper, to taste
- ½ cup shredded cheese (e.g., cheddar or Monterey Jack)
- Fresh cilantro, chopped (for garnish)

Instructions:

1. Preheat the oven to 375°F (190°C).
2. In a skillet, heat some oil over medium heat. Sauté the onions, minced garlic, and jalapeño pepper until they soften and become fragrant.
3. Add the cooked protein or vegetables to the skillet and season with ground cumin, salt, and pepper. Cook for a few minutes to combine the flavors.
4. Stir in the cooked rice and continue to cook for another few minutes. Remove from heat and let the filling cool slightly.
5. Stuff each bell pepper with the rice filling, pressing it down gently.
6. Place the stuffed bell peppers in a baking dish and cover the dish with aluminum foil.

7.	Bake in the preheated oven for 30 minutes.
8.	Remove the foil and sprinkle shredded cheese over the top of each bell pepper.
9.	Return the dish to the oven and bake for an additional 10-15 minutes, or until the cheese is melted and bubbly.
10.	Remove the Rice-stuffed Bell Peppers from the oven and let them cool for a few minutes.
11.	Garnish with chopped fresh cilantro and serve them warm.

These street food-inspired rice recipes bring the excitement of Mexican street food right into your own kitchen. Enjoy the flavors and textures of these portable and delicious creations that capture the essence of Mexican street food culture.

Chapter 7: Rice Soups and Stews

Rice plays a comforting and substantial role in Mexican soups and stews. In this chapter, we will explore a collection of rice-based soups and stews that are not only nourishing but also bursting with flavors that will warm your soul.

7.1 Sopa de Arroz (Mexican Rice Soup)

Sopa de Arroz, or Mexican Rice Soup, is a classic comfort food that combines the heartiness of rice with the flavors of vegetables and aromatic spices. This soup is a perfect option for a cozy and satisfying meal.

Ingredients:

- 1 cup long-grain white rice
- 2 tablespoons vegetable oil
- 1 small onion, finely chopped
- 2 cloves garlic, minced
- 2 carrots, peeled and diced
- 2 celery stalks, diced
- 4 cups chicken or vegetable broth
- 1 teaspoon ground cumin
- ½ teaspoon dried oregano
- Salt and pepper, to taste
- Fresh cilantro, chopped (for garnish)
- Lime wedges (for serving)

Instructions:

1. Rinse the rice under cold water until the water runs clear. Drain and set aside.
2. In a large pot, heat the vegetable oil over medium heat.

3. Add the chopped onion and minced garlic to the pot. Sauté until the onion becomes translucent and the garlic is fragrant.
4. Add the diced carrots and celery to the pot. Cook for a few minutes until they begin to soften.
5. Stir in the rinsed rice and cook for an additional 2-3 minutes, stirring constantly.
6. Pour in the chicken or vegetable broth, along with the ground cumin and dried oregano. Season with salt and pepper to taste.
7. Bring the soup to a boil, then reduce the heat to low and let it simmer for about 15-20 minutes, or until the rice is cooked and tender.
8. Adjust the seasoning if needed.
9. Ladle the Sopa de Arroz into bowls, garnish with fresh cilantro, and serve with lime wedges for squeezing over the soup.

7.2 Caldo de Res (Beef and Rice Soup)

Caldo de Res is a hearty beef and rice soup that is both nutritious and flavorful. Packed with tender beef, vegetables, and rice, this soup is a satisfying meal in itself.

Ingredients:

- 1 pound beef stew meat, cut into bite-sized pieces
- 2 tablespoons vegetable oil
- 1 onion, chopped
- 2 cloves garlic, minced
- 2 carrots, peeled and diced
- 2 potatoes, peeled and diced
- 2 celery stalks, diced
- 1 cup long-grain white rice
- 6 cups beef broth
- 1 bay leaf
- 1 teaspoon dried thyme
- Salt and pepper, to taste
- Fresh cilantro, chopped (for garnish)

Instructions:

1. In a large pot, heat the vegetable oil over medium heat.
2. Add the beef stew meat to the pot and cook until browned on all sides. Remove the meat from the pot and set aside.
3. In the same pot, add the chopped onion and minced garlic. Sauté until the onion becomes translucent and the garlic is fragrant.
4. Return the browned beef stew meat to the pot.
5. Add the diced carrots, potatoes, celery, rice, beef broth, bay leaf, and dried thyme to the pot. Season with salt and pepper to taste.
6. Bring the soup to a boil, then reduce the heat to low. Cover

and simmer for about 1 hour, or until the beef is tender and the flavors have melded together.

7. Adjust the seasoning if needed.
8. Ladle the Caldo de Res into bowls, garnish with fresh cilantro, and serve hot.

7.3 Pozole Rojo with Rice

Pozole Rojo with Rice is a rich and flavorful Mexican stew that combines tender meat, hearty hominy, and aromatic spices. The addition of rice adds a comforting and satisfying element to this traditional dish.

Ingredients:

- 1 cup long-grain white rice
- 2 tablespoons vegetable oil
- 1 onion, chopped
- 3 cloves garlic, minced
- 2 pounds pork shoulder, cut into bite-sized pieces
- 2 teaspoons ground cumin
- 1 teaspoon dried oregano
- ½ teaspoon chili powder
- 4 cups chicken broth
- 2 cups canned hominy, drained and rinsed
- Salt and pepper, to taste
- Toppings: chopped fresh cilantro, sliced radishes, shredded cabbage, lime wedges

Instructions:

1. Rinse the rice under cold water until the water runs clear. Drain and set aside.
2. In a large pot, heat the vegetable oil over medium heat.
3. Add the chopped onion and minced garlic to the pot. Sauté until the onion becomes translucent and the garlic is fragrant.
4. Add the pork shoulder pieces to the pot and cook until browned on all sides.
5. Stir in the ground cumin, dried oregano, and chili powder. Cook for a minute to toast the spices.
6. Add the rinsed rice to the pot and cook for an additional 2-3 minutes, stirring constantly.

7. Pour in the chicken broth and bring the mixture to a boil.
8. Reduce the heat to low, cover the pot, and simmer for about 30-40 minutes, or until the pork is tender and the rice is cooked.
9. Stir in the drained and rinsed hominy. Season with salt and pepper to taste.
10. Continue to simmer the Pozole Rojo for another 10 minutes to allow the flavors to meld together.
11. Adjust the seasoning if needed.
12. Serve the Pozole Rojo with Rice hot, garnished with chopped fresh cilantro, sliced radishes, shredded cabbage, and lime wedges.

7.4 Chicken and Rice Pozole

Chicken and Rice Pozole is a delightful twist on the traditional pozole, featuring tender chicken and rice in a flavorful and aromatic broth. This comforting soup is a perfect option for a satisfying and wholesome meal.

Ingredients:

- 1 cup long-grain white rice
- 2 tablespoons vegetable oil
- 1 onion, chopped
- 3 cloves garlic, minced
- 1 jalapeño pepper, seeds removed and finely chopped
- 1 teaspoon ground cumin
- ½ teaspoon dried oregano
- 4 cups chicken broth
- 2 cups cooked shredded chicken
- 2 cups canned hominy, drained and rinsed
- Salt and pepper, to taste

- Toppings: chopped fresh cilantro, sliced radishes, shredded cabbage, lime wedges

Instructions:

1. Rinse the rice under cold water until the water runs clear. Drain and set aside.
2. In a large pot, heat the vegetable oil over medium heat.
3. Add the chopped onion, minced garlic, and chopped jalapeño pepper to the pot. Sauté until the onion becomes translucent and the garlic is fragrant.
4. Stir in the ground cumin and dried oregano. Cook for a minute to toast the spices.
5. Add the rinsed rice to the pot and cook for an additional 2-3 minutes, stirring constantly.
6. Pour in the chicken broth and bring the mixture to a boil.
7. Reduce the heat to low, cover the pot, and simmer for about 15-20 minutes, or until the rice is cooked.
8. Stir in the cooked shredded chicken and drained hominy. Season with salt and pepper to taste.
9. Continue to simmer the Chicken and Rice Pozole for another 10 minutes to allow the flavors to meld together.
10. Adjust the seasoning if needed.
11. Serve the Chicken and Rice Pozole hot, garnished with chopped fresh cilantro, sliced radishes, shredded cabbage, and lime wedges.

These rice-based soups and stews are hearty, flavorful, and perfect for warming up on chilly days or anytime you crave a comforting bowl of goodness. Enjoy the richness and depth of flavors that these recipes bring to the table.

Chapter 8: Rice-based Casseroles and Bakes

Rice is a versatile ingredient that lends itself well to creating delicious and satisfying casseroles and bakes. In this chapter, we will explore a variety of Mexican-inspired rice-based casseroles and bakes that are sure to become family favorites.

8.1 Chiles Rellenos Casserole

Chiles Rellenos Casserole is a delightful twist on the classic stuffed pepper dish. This casserole combines roasted poblano peppers, cheesy rice filling, and a flavorful tomato sauce for a comforting and flavorful meal.

Ingredients:

- 4 large poblano peppers
- 2 cups cooked long-grain white rice
- 1 cup shredded cheese (e.g., Monterey Jack, cheddar)
- 1 cup corn kernels (fresh or frozen)
- 1 small onion, diced
- 2 cloves garlic, minced
- 1 teaspoon ground cumin
- Salt and pepper, to taste
- 1 (15-ounce) can tomato sauce
- 1 cup chicken or vegetable broth
- Fresh cilantro, chopped (for garnish)

Instructions:

1. Preheat the broiler in your oven.
2. Place the poblano peppers on a baking sheet and broil them for about 5 minutes on each side, or until the skins are blistered

and charred.

3. Remove the peppers from the oven and transfer them to a bowl. Cover the bowl with plastic wrap and let the peppers steam for about 10 minutes. This will help loosen the skins.

4. Once the peppers are cool enough to handle, peel off the skins and carefully remove the seeds and membranes. Set the peppers aside.

5. In a mixing bowl, combine the cooked rice, shredded cheese, corn kernels, diced onion, minced garlic, ground cumin, salt, and pepper. Mix well to combine.

6. Preheat the oven to 375°F (190°C).

7. In a baking dish, spread a thin layer of tomato sauce on the bottom.

8. Stuff each poblano pepper with the rice mixture and place them in the baking dish.

9. In a separate bowl, whisk together the remaining tomato sauce and chicken or vegetable broth. Season with salt and pepper to taste.

10. Pour the tomato sauce mixture over the stuffed peppers in the baking dish.

11. Cover the dish with aluminum foil and bake in the preheated oven for 25-30 minutes.

12. Remove the foil and continue to bake for an additional 10 minutes, or until the casserole is heated through and the cheese is melted and bubbly.

13. Garnish with fresh chopped cilantro and serve the Chiles Rellenos Casserole warm.

8.2 Enchilada Rice Casserole

Enchilada Rice Casserole brings together the flavors of traditional enchiladas and rice in a satisfying and easy-to-make dish. This casserole is layered with tortillas, rice, savory filling, and topped with enchilada sauce and cheese.

Ingredients:

- 2 cups cooked long-grain white rice
- 1 tablespoon vegetable oil
- 1 small onion, diced
- 2 cloves garlic, minced
- 1 bell pepper, diced
- 1 jalapeño pepper, seeds removed and finely chopped
- 1 teaspoon ground cumin
- 1 teaspoon chili powder
- Salt and pepper, to taste
- 1 (15-ounce) can black beans, drained and rinsed
- 1 (15-ounce) can corn kernels, drained
- 1 (10-ounce) can enchilada sauce
- 6 small corn tortillas
- 1 cup shredded cheese (e.g., Mexican blend, cheddar)
- Fresh cilantro, chopped (for garnish)

Instructions:

1. Preheat the oven to 375°F (190°C).
2. In a large skillet, heat the vegetable oil over medium heat.
3. Add the diced onion, minced garlic, bell pepper, and jalapeño pepper to the skillet. Sauté until the vegetables are tender.
4. Stir in the ground cumin, chili powder, salt, and pepper. Cook for an additional minute to toast the spices.
5. Add the cooked rice, black beans, and corn kernels to the skillet. Mix well to combine and heat through.
6. Grease a baking dish with cooking spray or oil.
7. Spread a thin layer of enchilada sauce on the bottom of the baking dish.
8. Place two corn tortillas on top of the sauce, overlapping them slightly.
9. Spoon half of the rice and vegetable mixture over the tortillas, spreading it evenly.
10. Drizzle some enchilada sauce over the rice layer.
11. Repeat the layers with the remaining tortillas, rice mixture, and enchilada sauce.
12. Sprinkle the shredded cheese evenly over the top of the casserole.
13. Cover the dish with aluminum foil and bake in the preheated oven for 20 minutes.
14. Remove the foil and continue to bake for an additional 10-15 minutes, or until the cheese is melted and golden.
15. Garnish with fresh chopped cilantro and serve the Enchilada Rice Casserole warm.

8.3 Chicken and Rice Enmoladas

Chicken and Rice Enmoladas combine the flavors of tender shredded chicken, savory rice, and rich mole sauce in a delightful and satisfying casserole. This dish is a celebration of Mexican cuisine and its complex flavors.

Ingredients:

- 2 cups cooked long-grain white rice
- 2 cups cooked shredded chicken
- 1 tablespoon vegetable oil
- 1 small onion, diced
- 2 cloves garlic, minced
- 1 teaspoon ground cumin
- 1 teaspoon chili powder
- Salt and pepper, to taste
- 1 cup mole sauce
- 6 small corn tortillas
- 1 cup shredded cheese (e.g., Mexican blend, Monterey Jack)
- Fresh cilantro, chopped (for garnish)

Instructions:

1. Preheat the oven to 375°F (190°C).
2. In a large skillet, heat the vegetable oil over medium heat.
3. Add the diced onion and minced garlic to the skillet. Sauté until the onion becomes translucent and the garlic is fragrant.
4. Stir in the ground cumin, chili powder, salt, and pepper. Cook for an additional minute to toast the spices.
5. Add the cooked rice and shredded chicken to the skillet. Mix well to combine and heat through.
6. Grease a baking dish with cooking spray or oil.
7. Spoon a thin layer of mole sauce onto the bottom of the baking dish.
8. Place two corn tortillas on top of the sauce, overlapping them slightly.
9. Spoon half of the chicken and rice mixture over the tortillas,

spreading it evenly.

10. Drizzle some mole sauce over the chicken and rice layer.
11. Repeat the layers with the remaining tortillas, chicken and rice mixture, and mole sauce.
12. Sprinkle the shredded cheese evenly over the top of the casserole.
13. Cover the dish with aluminum foil and bake in the preheated oven for 20 minutes.
14. Remove the foil and continue to bake for an additional 10-15 minutes, or until the cheese is melted and bubbly.
15. Garnish with fresh chopped cilantro and serve the Chicken and Rice Enmoladas warm.

8.4 Rice and Bean Bake

Rice and Bean Bake is a hearty and flavorful vegetarian dish that combines rice, beans, vegetables, and cheese into a satisfying casserole. This dish can be served as a main course or as a side dish to complement your favorite Mexican meal.

Ingredients:

- 2 cups cooked long-grain white rice
- 1 tablespoon vegetable oil
- 1 small onion, diced
- 2 cloves garlic, minced
- 1 bell pepper, diced
- 1 zucchini, diced
- 1 cup corn kernels (fresh or frozen)
- 1 (15-ounce) can black beans, drained and rinsed
- 1 (10-ounce) can diced tomatoes with green chilies, drained
- 1 teaspoon ground cumin
- 1 teaspoon chili powder
- Salt and pepper, to taste
- 1 cup shredded cheese (e.g., Mexican blend, cheddar)
- Fresh cilantro, chopped (for garnish)

Instructions:

1. Preheat the oven to 375°F (190°C).
2. In a large skillet, heat the vegetable oil over medium heat.
3. Add the diced onion, minced garlic, bell pepper, and zucchini to the skillet. Sauté until the vegetables are tender.
4. Stir in the cooked rice, corn kernels, black beans, diced tomatoes with green chilies, ground cumin, chili powder, salt, and pepper. Mix well to combine and heat through.
5. Grease a baking dish with cooking spray or oil.

6. Spread the rice and bean mixture evenly in the baking dish.
7. Sprinkle the shredded cheese over the top of the casserole.
8. Cover the dish with aluminum foil and bake in the preheated oven for 20 minutes.
9. Remove the foil and continue to bake for an additional 10-15 minutes, or until the cheese is melted and golden.
10. Garnish with fresh chopped cilantro and serve the Rice and Bean Bake warm.

These rice-based casseroles and bakes are sure to impress with their delicious flavors and comforting textures. Whether you're looking for a twist on a classic dish or a satisfying vegetarian option, these recipes have got you covered. Enjoy the delightful combination of rice, flavorsome fillings, and melty cheese in these crowd-pleasing casseroles and bakes.

Chapter 9: Festive and Holiday Rice Dishes

Rice plays a significant role in Mexican festive and holiday traditions. In this chapter, we will explore a selection of rice dishes that are perfect for celebrating special occasions and adding a touch of Mexican flair to your holiday gatherings.

9.1 Arroz Navideño (Christmas Rice)

Arroz Navideño, also known as Christmas Rice, is a festive and flavorful dish that is traditionally served during the holiday season in Mexico. It features a vibrant combination of ingredients that create a colorful and delicious rice dish.

Ingredients:

- 2 cups long-grain white rice
- 2 tablespoons vegetable oil
- 1 small onion, diced
- 2 cloves garlic, minced
- 1 red bell pepper, diced
- 1 green bell pepper, diced
- 1 carrot, diced
- 1 cup frozen peas
- 1 cup corn kernels (fresh or frozen)
- 3 cups chicken or vegetable broth
- 1 teaspoon ground cumin
- 1 teaspoon paprika
- Salt and pepper, to taste
- Fresh cilantro, chopped (for garnish)

Instructions:

1. Rinse the rice under cold water until the water runs clear.

Drain and set aside.
2. In a large skillet or pot, heat the vegetable oil over medium heat.
3. Add the diced onion and minced garlic to the skillet. Sauté until the onion becomes translucent and the garlic is fragrant.
4. Stir in the diced red and green bell peppers, carrot, frozen peas, and corn kernels. Cook for a few minutes until the vegetables begin to soften.
5. Add the rice to the skillet and stir to coat it with the vegetable mixture.
6. Pour in the chicken or vegetable broth, and season with ground cumin, paprika, salt, and pepper. Stir well to combine.
7. Bring the mixture to a boil, then reduce the heat to low. Cover the skillet and let the rice simmer for about 15-20 minutes, or until the rice is cooked and the liquid has been absorbed.
8. Remove the skillet from the heat and let the rice sit, covered, for a few minutes.
9. Fluff the rice with a fork and garnish with freshly chopped cilantro.
10. Serve the Arroz Navideño warm as a festive side dish for your Christmas celebrations.

9.2 Day of the Dead Rice

Day of the Dead, or Día de los Muertos, is a vibrant and colorful Mexican holiday that honors deceased loved ones. Day of the Dead Rice is a flavorful dish that is often prepared as part of the traditional offerings placed on altars and enjoyed during this festive time.

Ingredients:

- 2 cups long-grain white rice
- 2 tablespoons vegetable oil
- 1 small onion, diced
- 2 cloves garlic, minced
- 1 jalapeño pepper, seeds removed and finely chopped
- 1 cup tomato puree
- 3 cups chicken or vegetable broth
- 1 teaspoon ground cumin
- 1 teaspoon dried oregano
- Salt and pepper, to taste
- Fresh cilantro, chopped (for garnish)

Instructions:

1. Rinse the rice under cold water until the water runs clear. Drain and set aside.
2. In a large skillet or pot, heat the vegetable oil over medium heat.
3. Add the diced onion, minced garlic, and chopped jalapeño pepper to the skillet. Sauté until the onion becomes translucent and the garlic is fragrant.
4. Stir in the tomato puree and cook for a few minutes to develop the flavors.
5. Add the rice to the skillet and stir to coat it with the tomato mixture.
6. Pour in the chicken or vegetable broth, and season with ground

cumin, dried oregano, salt, and pepper. Stir well to combine.

7. Bring the mixture to a boil, then reduce the heat to low. Cover the skillet and let the rice simmer for about 15-20 minutes, or until the rice is cooked and the liquid has been absorbed.

8. Remove the skillet from the heat and let the rice sit, covered, for a few minutes.

9. Fluff the rice with a fork and garnish with freshly chopped cilantro.

10. Serve the Day of the Dead Rice as part of your Día de los Muertos celebrations or as a flavorful side dish.

9.3 Rice-stuffed Poblanos (Chiles en Nogada)

Chiles en Nogada is a traditional Mexican dish that is commonly prepared for Independence Day celebrations. This version features rice-stuffed poblanos, a delightful combination of flavors and textures that is sure to impress your guests.

Ingredients:

- 4 large poblano peppers
- 2 cups cooked long-grain white rice
- 1 tablespoon vegetable oil
- 1 small onion, diced
- 2 cloves garlic, minced
- 1 tomato, diced
- 1 cup cooked shredded chicken or beef (optional)
- 1/4 cup raisins
- 1/4 cup sliced almonds
- 1/4 cup chopped fresh parsley
- 1 teaspoon ground cinnamon
- 1/2 teaspoon ground cloves
- Salt and pepper, to taste
- 1 cup walnut sauce (salsa de nuez)
- Pomegranate seeds, for garnish

Instructions:

1. Preheat the broiler in your oven.
2. Place the poblano peppers on a baking sheet and broil them, turning occasionally, until the skin is blistered and charred. This process should take about 5-7 minutes.
3. Remove the peppers from the oven and transfer them to a plastic bag. Seal the bag and let the peppers steam for about 10 minutes. This will make it easier to remove the skin.
4. After the peppers have cooled slightly, carefully peel off the

skin. Make a lengthwise slit on each pepper and remove the seeds and membranes, being careful not to tear the peppers.

5. In a large skillet, heat the vegetable oil over medium heat.
6. Add the diced onion and minced garlic to the skillet. Sauté until the onion becomes translucent and the garlic is fragrant.
7. Stir in the diced tomato, cooked rice, shredded chicken or beef (if using), raisins, sliced almonds, chopped fresh parsley, ground cinnamon, ground cloves, salt, and pepper. Mix well to combine.
8. Stuff the poblano peppers with the rice mixture, gently pressing it in to fill the cavity.
9. Place the stuffed peppers on a baking dish and spoon the walnut sauce over them.
10. Bake in a preheated oven at 375°F (190°C) for about 15-20 minutes, or until the peppers are heated through and the flavors have melded together.
11. Remove from the oven and garnish with pomegranate seeds.
12. Serve the Rice-stuffed Poblanos (Chiles en Nogada) as a festive main course for your special holiday celebrations.

9.4 Traditional Rice Tamales

Tamales are a beloved Mexican dish made of masa (corn dough) filled with various ingredients and wrapped in corn husks. Traditional Rice Tamales are a simple yet delicious variation that highlight the flavors of the masa and rice.

Ingredients:

- 2 cups masa harina (corn flour)
- 1 1/2 cups chicken or vegetable broth
- 1/2 cup vegetable shortening or lard
- 1 teaspoon baking powder
- 1/2 teaspoon salt
- 1 1/2 cups cooked long-grain white rice
- Corn husks, soaked in warm water for about 30 minutes

Instructions:

1. In a large mixing bowl, combine the masa harina, chicken or vegetable broth, vegetable shortening or lard, baking powder, and salt. Mix well until a smooth dough forms.
2. Drain the corn husks from the water and pat them dry.
3. Take a soaked corn husk and spread a thin layer of the masa dough on the wider end of the husk, leaving a border around the edges.
4. Place a spoonful of cooked rice in the center of the masa dough.
5. Fold the sides of the corn husk toward the center, enclosing the rice and forming a neat package. Fold the bottom of the husk up to seal the tamale.
6. Repeat the process with the remaining corn husks, masa dough, and rice.
7. Arrange the tamales in a steamer basket, standing them upright with the folded ends facing down.

8. Fill the bottom of a large pot with water, making sure the water level is below the steamer basket.

9. Place the pot on the stove over medium heat and bring the water to a simmer.

10. Cover the pot and steam the tamales for about 1-1.5 hours, or until the masa is firm and cooked through.

11. Remove the tamales from the steamer and let them cool for a few minutes before unwrapping.

12. Serve the Traditional Rice Tamales warm as a delightful addition to your festive holiday table.

These festive and holiday rice dishes showcase the rich culinary traditions of Mexico during special occasions. From the vibrant Arroz Navideño to the flavorful Chiles en Nogada, these recipes will bring joy and deliciousness to your celebrations. Embrace the festive spirit and indulge in these delightful rice dishes that are sure to become holiday favorites.

Chapter 10: Rice Desserts and Sweet Treats

Rice is not only versatile in savory dishes but also shines in delectable desserts and sweet treats. In this chapter, we will explore a selection of delightful rice-based desserts that will satisfy your sweet tooth and leave you craving for more.

10.1 Horchata Rice Pudding

Horchata Rice Pudding is a creamy and comforting dessert that combines the flavors of horchata, a popular Mexican rice-based drink, with the classic rice pudding. It's a delightful treat that is perfect for indulging in after a satisfying meal.

Ingredients:

- 1 cup long-grain white rice
- 4 cups milk
- 1 cinnamon stick
- 1/2 cup granulated sugar
- 1 teaspoon vanilla extract
- Ground cinnamon, for garnish

Instructions:

1. Rinse the rice under cold water until the water runs clear. Drain and set aside.
2. In a large saucepan, combine the rice, milk, and cinnamon stick.
3. Bring the mixture to a boil over medium-high heat, then reduce the heat to low.
4. Simmer the rice mixture, stirring occasionally, for about 20-25 minutes, or until the rice is cooked and tender.
5. Stir in the granulated sugar and vanilla extract. Continue to

cook for another 5 minutes, stirring occasionally.

6. Remove the cinnamon stick from the rice pudding.
7. Transfer the rice pudding to serving bowls or glasses.
8. Sprinkle ground cinnamon on top for garnish.
9. Serve the Horchata Rice Pudding warm or chilled, depending on your preference.

10.2 Arroz con Leche Ice Cream

Arroz con Leche Ice Cream is a delightful frozen treat that captures the creamy and comforting flavors of the traditional Mexican rice pudding. It's a perfect dessert for hot summer days or whenever you crave a refreshing and indulgent ice cream experience.

Ingredients:

- 2 cups cooked long-grain white rice
- 2 cups whole milk
- 1 cup heavy cream
- 1/2 cup granulated sugar
- 1 teaspoon vanilla extract
- Ground cinnamon, for garnish

Instructions:

1. In a blender or food processor, combine the cooked rice, whole milk, heavy cream, granulated sugar, and vanilla extract.
2. Blend the mixture until smooth and well combined.
3. Pour the mixture into an ice cream maker and churn according to the manufacturer's instructions.
4. Once the ice cream reaches the desired consistency, transfer it to a lidded container and freeze for a few hours to firm up.
5. When ready to serve, scoop the Arroz con Leche Ice Cream into bowls or cones.
6. Sprinkle ground cinnamon on top for an extra touch of flavor and garnish.
7. Enjoy the creamy and delightful Arroz con Leche Ice Cream as a refreshing dessert.

10.3 Caramelized Rice Flan

Caramelized Rice Flan is a decadent and elegant dessert that combines the smooth and creamy texture of flan with the subtle flavor of rice. It's a show-stopping treat that will impress your guests and leave them wanting more.

Ingredients:

- 1 cup cooked long-grain white rice
- 1 cup granulated sugar, divided
- 4 eggs
- 2 cups whole milk
- 1 teaspoon vanilla extract
- Pinch of salt

Instructions:

1. Preheat the oven to 350°F (175°C).
2. In a small saucepan, melt 1/2 cup of granulated sugar over medium heat, stirring constantly until it turns golden brown and caramelizes.
3. Quickly pour the caramelized sugar into a flan mold or individual ramekins, swirling to coat the bottom evenly. Be careful as the caramel will be very hot.
4. In a blender or food processor, combine the cooked rice, eggs, whole milk, remaining 1/2 cup of granulated sugar, vanilla extract, and salt. Blend until smooth and well combined.
5. Pour the rice mixture into the flan mold or ramekins with the caramelized sugar.
6. Place the flan mold or ramekins in a baking dish filled with hot water, creating a water bath.
7. Carefully transfer the baking dish to the preheated oven and bake for about 45-50 minutes, or until the flan is set and slightly jiggly in the center.
8. Remove the flan from the oven and let it cool to room temperature.
9. Once cooled, refrigerate the flan for at least 2 hours or

overnight to chill and firm up.

10. To serve, run a knife around the edges of the flan mold or ramekins to loosen the caramelized rice flan. Invert onto a serving plate, allowing the caramel sauce to drizzle over the flan.

11. Slice and serve the Caramelized Rice Flan as an elegant and indulgent dessert.

10.4 Rice Krispies Mexican Treats

Rice Krispies Mexican Treats are a fun and playful twist on the classic Rice Krispies treats, infused with Mexican flavors and a touch of spice. These treats are easy to make and perfect for parties, gatherings, or simply enjoying as a sweet snack.

Ingredients:

- 3 tablespoons unsalted butter
- 4 cups mini marshmallows
- 1 teaspoon vanilla extract
- 1 teaspoon ground cinnamon
- 1/4 teaspoon chili powder (optional, for a spicy kick)
- 6 cups Rice Krispies cereal
- Mini chocolate chips, for garnish (optional)

Instructions:

1. In a large saucepan, melt the unsalted butter over low heat.
2. Add the mini marshmallows to the saucepan and stir until completely melted and smooth.
3. Stir in the vanilla extract, ground cinnamon, and chili powder (if using), mixing well to incorporate the flavors.
4. Remove the saucepan from the heat and add the Rice Krispies cereal. Stir until the cereal is evenly coated with the marshmallow mixture.
5. Lightly grease a baking dish or line it with parchment paper.
6. Transfer the Rice Krispies mixture to the baking dish and press it down evenly using a spatula or your hands.
7. Sprinkle mini chocolate chips on top for an optional garnish, gently pressing them into the treats.
8. Allow the treats to cool and set at room temperature for about 1 hour.
9. Once cooled and set, cut the Rice Krispies Mexican Treats into

squares or desired shapes.

10. Serve these delightful and flavorful treats as a sweet and crunchy snack.

Indulge in the deliciousness of these rice-based desserts and sweet treats, ranging from creamy and comforting rice pudding to refreshing ice cream, elegant caramelized flan, and playful Rice Krispies treats. These recipes will satisfy your dessert cravings and add a touch of sweetness to any occasion. Enjoy the wonderful world of rice desserts!

Chapter 11: Modern and Fusion Rice Creations

In this chapter, we will explore modern and fusion rice creations that blend Mexican flavors with international influences, resulting in unique and delicious dishes that will surprise and delight your taste buds.

11.1 Mexican Rice Sushi Rolls

Mexican Rice Sushi Rolls combine the traditional flavors of sushi with a Mexican twist. These rolls feature seasoned Mexican rice, fresh vegetables, and a variety of fillings, wrapped in nori seaweed sheets. They are a creative and colorful take on sushi that will impress your guests and bring a unique fusion of flavors to your table.

Ingredients:

- Nori seaweed sheets
- Cooked sushi rice seasoned with a Mexican twist (such as adding lime juice and cilantro)
- Assorted fillings (e.g., avocado, cucumber, cooked shrimp, sliced jalapeños, pickled vegetables)
- Soy sauce and wasabi, for serving

Instructions:

1. Place a sheet of nori seaweed on a bamboo sushi mat or a clean surface.
2. Spread a thin, even layer of seasoned sushi rice on the nori, leaving a small border at the top.
3. Arrange your desired fillings in a line across the center of the rice.
4. Using the bamboo mat or your hands, carefully roll the sushi tightly, starting from the bottom, and applying gentle pressure to ensure a compact roll.

5. Wet the top border of the nori with a little water to seal the roll.
6. Repeat the process with the remaining ingredients.
7. Slice the sushi rolls into bite-sized pieces using a sharp knife.
8. Serve the Mexican Rice Sushi Rolls with soy sauce and wasabi for dipping.

11.2 Rice-stuffed Peppers with Quinoa

Rice-stuffed Peppers with Quinoa are a flavorful and nutritious dish that combines the classic stuffed pepper concept with the addition of quinoa, a protein-packed grain. The result is a hearty and satisfying meal that is both delicious and wholesome.

Ingredients:

- Bell peppers (any color), tops removed and seeds removed
- Cooked rice (white or brown)
- Cooked quinoa
- Sautéed vegetables (e.g., onions, garlic, zucchini, corn, black beans)
- Shredded cheese (such as cheddar or Mexican blend)
- Fresh herbs (e.g., cilantro, parsley) for garnish
- Salt, pepper, and spices (such as cumin and chili powder) to taste

Instructions:

1. Preheat the oven to 375°F (190°C).
2. In a large mixing bowl, combine the cooked rice, cooked quinoa, sautéed vegetables, shredded cheese, and seasonings. Mix well to incorporate all the ingredients.
3. Stuff each bell pepper with the rice-quinoa filling, pressing it down gently.
4. Place the stuffed peppers in a baking dish and cover with foil.
5. Bake the peppers in the preheated oven for about 25-30 minutes, or until the peppers are tender and the filling is heated through.
6. Remove the foil and continue baking for an additional 5-10 minutes to allow the cheese to melt and slightly brown.
7. Garnish the rice-stuffed peppers with fresh herbs.
8. Serve the peppers as a delicious and wholesome main course.

11.3 Tex-Mex Rice and Beans Bowl

Tex-Mex Rice and Beans Bowl is a flavorful and satisfying one-bowl meal that combines Mexican-inspired rice, seasoned beans, fresh toppings, and a zesty dressing. It's a versatile dish that allows for customization and is perfect for a quick and nutritious lunch or dinner.

Ingredients:

- Cooked Mexican-style rice (seasoned with spices like cumin, paprika, and chili powder)
- Cooked black beans or pinto beans, seasoned with garlic, cumin, and salt
- Fresh toppings (e.g., diced tomatoes, sliced avocado, chopped cilantro, diced red onion)
- Lime wedges, for serving
- Zesty dressing (e.g., a mixture of lime juice, olive oil, minced garlic, and honey)

Instructions:

1. In a serving bowl, layer the cooked Mexican-style rice and seasoned beans.
2. Top with your desired fresh toppings, such as diced tomatoes, sliced avocado, chopped cilantro, and diced red onion.
3. Drizzle the zesty dressing over the bowl, or serve it on the side.
4. Squeeze fresh lime juice over the bowl for an extra burst of flavor.
5. Toss the ingredients together before eating, ensuring that the flavors are evenly distributed.
6. Enjoy the Tex-Mex Rice and Beans Bowl as a satisfying and nutritious meal.

11.4 Mexican Rice Pizza

Mexican Rice Pizza combines the beloved flavors of Mexican cuisine with the comfort and convenience of pizza. This fusion dish features a crispy tortilla crust topped with seasoned Mexican rice, vibrant vegetables, melted cheese, and a variety of Mexican-inspired toppings. It's a fun and delicious twist on traditional pizza that will spice up your pizza nights.

Ingredients:

1. Large tortilla or pre-made pizza crust
2. Cooked Mexican-style rice (seasoned with spices like cumin, paprika, and chili powder)
3. Salsa or tomato sauce
4. Shredded cheese (such as Monterey Jack, cheddar, or Mexican blend)
5. Assorted toppings (e.g., sliced bell peppers, diced onions, sliced jalapeños, black olives, cooked chicken or beef)
6. Fresh cilantro, for garnish

Instructions:

1. Preheat the oven to the temperature recommended for your pizza crust or tortilla.
2. Place the tortilla or pre-made pizza crust on a baking sheet or pizza stone.
3. Spread a layer of salsa or tomato sauce over the crust, leaving a small border around the edges.
4. Spread the cooked Mexican-style rice evenly over the sauce.
5. Sprinkle a generous amount of shredded cheese over the rice.
6. Add your desired toppings, such as sliced bell peppers, diced onions, sliced jalapeños, black olives, and cooked chicken or beef.
7. Bake the Mexican Rice Pizza in the preheated oven for the recommended time, or until the crust is crispy and the cheese is

melted and bubbly.

8. Remove the pizza from the oven and garnish with fresh cilantro.

9. Slice and serve the Mexican Rice Pizza as a delightful and flavorful fusion dish.

Explore the exciting world of modern and fusion rice creations with these unique recipes. From Mexican Rice Sushi Rolls to Rice-stuffed Peppers with Quinoa, Tex-Mex Rice and Beans Bowl, and Mexican Rice Pizza, these dishes bring together the best of Mexican flavors and international influences. Enjoy the fusion of tastes and textures in these modern rice creations!

Chapter 12: Tips and Techniques for Perfect Mexican Rice

In this chapter, we will dive into the essential tips and techniques that will help you master the art of making perfect Mexican rice. From toasting the rice for maximum flavor to achieving the right texture and consistency, as well as exploring various seasoning and spice combinations, and learning the best practices for storage and reheating, these tips will elevate your Mexican rice cooking skills to the next level.

12.1 Preparing and Toasting Rice for Maximum Flavor

Toasting the rice before cooking is a crucial step that adds depth and nuttiness to the flavor of Mexican rice. Follow these steps to achieve maximum flavor:

Rinse the rice: Rinse the rice under cold water until the water runs clear. This removes excess starch and helps prevent clumping.

Dry the rice: Drain the rinsed rice well and spread it out on a clean kitchen towel or paper towel. Allow it to air dry for about 10-15 minutes. This step helps the rice to toast evenly.

Heat the oil: In a large skillet or saucepan, heat a tablespoon of oil over medium heat.

Add the rice: Once the oil is hot, add the dried rice to the skillet. Stir the rice continuously to coat each grain with oil and toast it evenly.

Toast until golden: Continue stirring the rice over medium heat until it turns a light golden color. Be careful not to burn it. This toasting process enhances the flavor and gives the rice a nutty aroma.

12.2 Achieving the Right Texture and Consistency

The texture and consistency of Mexican rice are key to its success. Follow these tips to achieve perfectly cooked rice:

Proper liquid-to-rice ratio: The general rule of thumb is to use 1 ¾ cups of liquid (water or broth) for every 1 cup of rice. Adjust the liquid quantity as needed based on the specific type of rice you're using.

Simmer and steam: Once you've added the liquid to the toasted rice, bring it to a boil, then reduce the heat to low and cover the pot. Allow the rice to simmer gently for the recommended cooking time specified on the rice package. Avoid lifting the lid during this time, as it will disrupt the steaming process.

Fluff with a fork: After the cooking time is complete, remove the pot from the heat and let it sit, covered, for an additional 5-10 minutes. This resting period allows the rice to steam and absorb any remaining moisture. Then, fluff the rice with a fork to separate the grains.

Adjust moisture level: If the rice seems too dry, sprinkle a little extra liquid (water or broth) over the rice and gently mix it in with a fork. If it appears too moist, leave the lid off for a few minutes to allow excess moisture to evaporate.

12.3 Seasoning and Spice Combinations

The right seasoning and spice combinations can elevate the flavor of Mexican rice. Experiment with the following options to find your preferred taste:

Garlic and onion: Sauté minced garlic and diced onion in the oil before adding the rice. This adds aromatic flavor to the dish.

Tomato-based seasonings: Include tomato sauce, tomato paste, or diced tomatoes with their juices to add a rich, tangy flavor and vibrant color to the rice.

Spice blends: Use a combination of spices like cumin, chili powder, paprika, oregano, and coriander to enhance the Mexican flavors. Adjust the amounts according to your taste preferences.

Fresh herbs: Add fresh herbs like cilantro or parsley at the end of cooking for a burst of freshness and added aroma.

12.4 Storage and Reheating Recommendations

If you have leftover Mexican rice, follow these storage and reheating recommendations to preserve its quality:

Cool and refrigerate: Allow the rice to cool completely before transferring it to an airtight container. Refrigerate it promptly to prevent bacterial growth.

Reheat on the stovetop: To reheat refrigerated rice, add a small amount of liquid (water or broth) to a saucepan and warm it over medium heat. Add the rice to the pan and stir occasionally until heated through.

Steam reheating: Place the refrigerated rice in a heatproof bowl and cover it with a damp paper towel. Steam the rice in a steamer basket or a pot with a tight-fitting lid over simmering water until it's heated thoroughly.

Avoid microwave reheating: While the microwave is a convenient option, reheating rice in the microwave can result in uneven heating and a loss of texture. If you choose to use the microwave, add a little water to the rice and cover it with a microwave-safe lid or plastic wrap to create steam.

By following these tips and techniques, you'll be able to achieve perfect Mexican rice every time. From toasting the rice for maximum flavor to achieving the right texture and consistency, and experimenting with seasoning and spice combinations, as well as properly storing and reheating leftovers, you'll become a master of Mexican rice cooking. Enjoy the delicious flavors and aromas that these techniques bring to your rice dishes!

Chapter 13: Beyond the Rice: Complementary Mexican Dishes

In this final chapter, we will explore a variety of complementary Mexican dishes that pair perfectly with Mexican rice. These dishes will enhance your culinary experience and bring a complete Mexican feast to your table. From guacamole and salsa variations to traditional Mexican sides and appetizers, refreshing agua fresca recipes, and Mexican-inspired cocktails and mocktails, these recipes will add a delightful touch to your Mexican rice meals.

13.1 Guacamole and Salsa Variations

Guacamole and salsa are iconic Mexican condiments that bring vibrant flavors and freshness to any meal. Try these variations to add excitement to your Mexican rice dishes:

Classic Guacamole: Mash ripe avocados with lime juice, diced tomatoes, minced garlic, chopped cilantro, and salt. Adjust the ingredients to achieve your preferred level of spice and tanginess.

Mango Salsa: Combine diced mango, red onion, jalapeño peppers, fresh lime juice, chopped cilantro, and a pinch of salt. This sweet and spicy salsa pairs well with the savory flavors of Mexican rice.

Pico de Gallo: Mix together diced tomatoes, onions, jalapeño peppers, fresh lime juice, chopped cilantro, and salt. The freshness of pico de gallo adds a zesty kick to your rice dishes.

Roasted Corn Salsa: Roast fresh corn kernels until slightly charred, then combine them with diced red bell pepper, red onion, jalapeño peppers, lime juice, cilantro, and a touch of salt. The smoky and sweet flavors of this salsa create a delicious contrast with Mexican rice.

13.2 Traditional Mexican Sides and Appetizers

Complete your Mexican rice feast with these traditional sides and appetizers that are bursting with authentic flavors:

Refried Beans: Cook pinto or black beans until soft, then mash them with garlic, onion, and spices. Sauté the mixture in oil until creamy and serve as a hearty and flavorful side dish.

Mexican Street Corn (Elote): Grill or roast corn on the cob, then slather it with a mixture of mayonnaise, lime juice, chili powder, and crumbled cheese (such as cotija). Sprinkle with chopped cilantro and enjoy the irresistible combination of smoky, tangy, and creamy flavors.

Quesadillas: Fill tortillas with a variety of cheeses, cooked chicken, beef, or sautéed vegetables. Cook them on a griddle or in a skillet until the cheese is melted and the tortillas are golden and crispy. Slice into wedges and serve as a satisfying appetizer or side dish.

Tamales: Steam homemade or store-bought tamales filled with various fillings like pork, chicken, cheese, or vegetables. Tamales are a traditional Mexican delicacy that adds richness and diversity to your Mexican rice meal.

13.3 Refreshing Agua Fresca Recipes

Agua frescas are refreshing fruit-based beverages that are popular in Mexico. They provide a cooling and thirst-quenching accompaniment to your Mexican rice dishes. Try these easy and delicious agua fresca recipes:

Watermelon Agua Fresca: Blend fresh watermelon chunks with water, a squeeze of lime juice, and a touch of sweetener (optional). Strain the mixture, and serve over ice for a sweet and hydrating drink.

Pineapple Agua Fresca: Blend ripe pineapple chunks with water, lime juice, and a hint of honey or agave syrup. Strain the mixture, and serve over ice for a tropical and tangy beverage.

Cucumber-Lime Agua Fresca: Blend peeled and chopped cucumbers with water, lime juice, a touch of sweetener, and a few fresh mint leaves. Strain the mixture, and serve chilled for a revitalizing and refreshing drink.

Hibiscus (Jamaica) Agua Fresca: Steep dried hibiscus flowers in hot water with a bit of sugar until a deep red infusion is achieved. Strain and cool the liquid, then serve over ice for a tart and floral drink.

13.4 Mexican-Inspired Cocktails and Mocktails

For those looking to add a festive touch to their Mexican rice meals, these cocktails and mocktails are perfect choices:

Margarita: Mix tequila, fresh lime juice, and orange liqueur in a shaker with ice. Shake well and strain into a salt-rimmed glass. Garnish with a lime wedge for a classic and refreshing Mexican cocktail.

Paloma: Combine tequila, fresh grapefruit juice, lime juice, and a splash of soda water. Serve over ice with a grapefruit wedge for a tangy and bubbly cocktail.

Virgin Piña Colada: Blend pineapple juice, coconut milk, and ice until smooth. Pour into a glass and garnish with a pineapple slice and a maraschino cherry for a tropical and non-alcoholic treat.

Agua de Jamaica Cocktail: Mix hibiscus (jamaica) agua fresca with tequila, a splash of lime juice, and a touch of sweetener. Serve over ice and garnish with a lime wedge for a vibrant and flavorful cocktail.

By exploring the world of guacamole and salsa variations, traditional Mexican sides and appetizers, refreshing agua fresca recipes, and Mexican-inspired cocktails and mocktails, you'll enhance the flavors and enjoyment of your Mexican rice dishes. These complementary dishes will complete your Mexican culinary experience and leave your taste buds satisfied. Cheers to a delicious and vibrant Mexican feast!

Conclusion

Congratulations! You have completed your culinary journey through the "Mexican Rice Cookbook 101." Throughout this cookbook, we have explored the rich and diverse world of Mexican rice, discovering traditional recipes, modern creations, and a variety of complementary dishes that elevate the dining experience.

From the aromatic and flavorful Arroz Rojo (Red Rice) to the zesty and refreshing Cilantro Lime Rice, from the hearty and comforting Arroz con Pollo (Chicken and Rice) to the indulgent and sweet Horchata Rice Pudding, this cookbook has provided you with a wide array of rice dishes to satisfy every craving and occasion.

You have learned about the history and cultural significance of Mexican rice, essential ingredients and equipment, and tips and techniques to achieve perfect results. The chapters have taken you on a culinary adventure, showcasing the versatility of rice in Mexican cuisine and the various ways it can be flavored, paired, and transformed into mouthwatering creations.

Remember to embrace the vibrant flavors of Mexico by preparing delicious guacamole and salsa variations, exploring traditional sides and appetizers, and indulging in refreshing agua frescas and Mexican-inspired cocktails or mocktails. These complementary dishes add depth, variety, and a festive touch to your Mexican rice meals, creating a complete dining experience.

So grab your apron, gather your ingredients, and embark on the journey of creating delightful Mexican rice dishes. Whether you're cooking for yourself, your family, or entertaining guests, this cookbook will be your guide to mastering the art of Mexican rice cooking.

Enjoy the wonderful flavors, aromas, and textures that Mexican cuisine has to offer. May your kitchen be filled with the spirit of Mexico as you embark on this culinary adventure. Buen provecho!